Jesus Loves Me

By: Daniel Tirado

We love him, because he first loved us.

— 1 John 4:19 —

APOSTOLIC

PRESS, INC.

Giving Thanks!

I want to thank my God and Savior, Jesus Christ, who loved me first. I want to thank my Pastor, Joel Booker and Bishop, Larry Booker who inspired me to finish this book. And my family who supported me each and every the step of the way, helped, and encouraged me.

There was a little boy named Timmy.

He was a curious and adventurous child, always eager to explore the world around him.

One day, as Timmy was exploring the woods behind his grandparent's farm, he came across a beautiful flower garden.

As he walked through the garden, Timmy couldn't help but wonder who could have created such a beautiful place.

He looked up at the sky and said, "Jesus, are you the one who made this garden?"

Just then, a gentle breeze blew through the trees, rustling the leaves and making the flowers sway.

Timmy smiled and knew that Jesus was with him.

He spent the whole day in the garden, marveling at the beauty of the flowers and the way they seemed to dance in the sunshine.

As he was leaving the garden, He came across a small bird with a broken wing. The bird was standing on the ground, unable to fly.

Timmy felt sad for the little bird and decided to take it home with him to care for it.

When Timmy got home, he made a little nest for the bird and gave it some water and food.

The blue jay was so grateful to Timmy for helping it, and soon its wing was healed, and it was able to fly again.

Timmy was glad that he could help the bird and knew that it was Jesus who had guided him to the garden and helped him to care for the bird.

He realized that Jesus loved him very much and that He was always with him, because nothing can separate us from His love.

From that day on, Timmy knew that no matter where he went or what he did, Jesus would always be there to love and protect him.

And he was so happy because he knew he was loved by God, the most powerful force in the world.

In this story, we learn that God's love is greater than anything in this world, and nothing can separate us from the love of God.

And just like Timmy, you can trust that Jesus loves you, and we can always pray and talk to Him like a friend.

Made in the USA
Las Vegas, NV
29 January 2024

85054312R00017